G000153724

Robin Gill held the Michael Ramsey Chair of Modern Theology in the University of Kent, Canterbury, for 20 years. Since 2013, he has been Emeritus Professor of Applied Theology there. For 13 years, he was the chair of the Archbishop of Canterbury's Medical Ethics Advisory Group. He is Honorary Provincial Canon of Canterbury Cathedral and Canon Theologian at Gibraltar Cathedral. He is the editor of the journal *Theology* and the Cambridge University Press monograph series, *New Studies in Christian Ethics*. Previously, he held the William Leech Research Chair of Applied Theology at the University of Newcastle. He is the author or editor of some forty books, including *Health Care and Christian Ethics* (Cambridge University Press, 2007). His most recent are *Theology in a Social Context: Sociological theology volume 1, Theology Shaped by Society: Sociological theology volume 2* and *Society Shaped by Theology: Sociological theology volume 3* (Ashgate, 2012–13), *A Textbook of Christian Ethics* (4th edn, T&T Clark, 2014) and *Moral Passion and Christian Ethics* (Cambridge University Press, 2017).

Little Books of Guidance
Finding answers to life's big questions!

Also in the series:

WHY BE GOOD?

A little book of guidance

ROBIN GILL

First published in Great Britain in 2016

Society for Promoting Christian Knowledge
36 Causton Street
London SW1P 4ST
www.spck.org.uk

The author and publisher have made every effort to ensure that the external
website and email addresses included in this book are correct and up to date
at the time of going to press. The author and publisher are not responsible
for the content, quality or continuing accessibility of the sites.

Scripture quotations are taken from the New Revised Standard Version of
the Bible, Anglicized Edition, copyright © 1989, 1995 by the Division
of Christian Education of the National Council of the Churches of
Christ in the USA. Used by permission. All rights reserved.

British Library Cataloguing-in-Publication Data
A catalogue record for this book is available from the British Library

ISBN 978–0–281–07656–7
eBook ISBN 978–0–281–07657–4

Typeset by Graphicraft Limited, Hong Kong
First printed in Great Britain by Ashford Colour Press
Subsequently digitally printed in Great Britain

eBook by Graphicraft Limited, Hong Kong

Produced on paper from sustainable forests

Contents

Introduction

This Little Book of Guidance seeks to address the question 'Why be good?' It may not be apparent that we need to give an answer to this question. Many might consider it obvious that we should all try to be good. After all, even criminals typically have a code of good conduct among themselves – if only a code that they do not betray, and do show respect to, other criminals. Trying to be good might seem to be a basic human instinct that does not need to be explained.

Perhaps it is. But the trouble is that not all human 'instincts' are good. Males forcing themselves sexually upon females seems to be instinctive for many mammals, but is now regarded as rape in most human societies. Again, males killing the offspring of new females that they desire is common among lions and tigers – and even among some of our nearest living relatives, chimpanzees – but is regarded as murder among humans. Instinct is not always a reliable guide to goodness.

Instead of relying upon instinct, I am going to explore four possible answers. We should be good:

- because some things are evil;
- because if I scratch your back you will scratch mine;
- because it is our duty;
- because God is good.

This list is certainly not exhaustive. I am sure that you can think of plenty of other possible reasons. For example:

- because it will make you happy;
- because you will be rewarded in heaven;
- because, if you are not good, you will go to hell.

Later I will offer examples of human goodness that bring little or no personal happiness to the actors involved. Of course it is possible to overcome that problem simply by equating goodness and happiness. On that account everything that makes us happy is good and everything that does not is not good. Personal happiness and goodness is one and the same thing. Much depends here upon how 'happiness' is defined. At its most simplistic it could be defined as 'what gives us pleasure'. So, if something gives me pleasure, then it is good. Unfortunately some people seem to derive pleasure from torturing, or being tortured by, other people. Most of us would not regard such people as good in any meaningful sense of the term.

Being rewarded in heaven or escaping punishments in hell (or for Hindus, and some Buddhists, escaping the burdensome cycle of re-birth) have often been used by religious people as reasons for being good. The Victorians, in particular, agonized about whether a decline in belief of eternal punishments in hell (a decline that they were already experiencing) would lead to a breakdown in morality. A fear of hell, so some argued, was a strong incentive for people to be good in this life. There are already plenty of books following this line of argument, but this Little Book of Guidance is not going to be one of them. I have always regarded rewards in heaven or punishments in hell as dubious, amoral reasons for being good. Such punishments/rewards may be effective incentives for those still convinced about the reality of eternal punishments in hell, but they are poor reasons for being good. In their terms, being good is simply a product of fear and not of love or compassion. And they are many miles away from the loving God that I believe in. So I will pursue them no further. Other people can do so if they wish.

Instead I will explore three non-religious reasons for being good before I come to the fourth reason, namely 'because God is good'. This is deliberate because, emphatically, I do not wish to give any impression that only religious people can justify being good, let alone that only religious people can actually be good. Some religious people argue that without a belief in God there can be no morality. But I am not one of them. I spend much of my professional life discussing medical ethics with doctors and nurses of different faiths and of no-faith (or, more accurately, of no-explicitly-religious faith). I am keen for them all to think and act ethically, whether they think of themselves as religious or not. And I have seen plenty of evidence of goodness among doctors and nurses who profess no-faith. I am also persuaded that some religious people in the past, and sadly some still in the present, have been appallingly evil. Exclusive religious claims to goodness just do not seem to me to be credible.

Nevertheless I will come to the role of faith in the final chapter, exploring a few of the human implications of a belief that God is good – a belief that is central to Judaism, Christianity and Islam. I am conscious that

I will not often explore those forms of religious belief, such as Theravada Buddhism, where God is absent, let alone Confucianism, which may or may not be counted as religious. That would take me too far out of my area of competence and here, too, I will leave that for others to explore. Instead I will focus upon the three so-called Abrahamic faiths – Judaism, Christianity and Islam – that are particularly prevalent and influential in Western society. Within these three traditions does a belief that God is good give their followers, not a monopoly of goodness, but an important extra reason for being good?

1

Because some things are evil

Alex Garland's much praised 2015 film *Ex Machina* concludes with a moral dilemma. From the outset the film is concerned to test whether a humanoid robot, played with aplomb by the Swedish actress Alicia Vikander, can pass the test of being able to think for itself. Slowly it becomes evident that this human artefact can indeed do so and is fully sentient. But is it/she actually moral? In the much-debated final scene the robot appears to kill not just the scientist who had created and then threatened to destroy her, but also the well-meaning visitor who has fallen in love with her and has just helped her to escape. Apparently she kills without any moral discrimination. She may well be sentient but it is not evident that she is actually moral.

Fans of the film debate whether or not the visitor might actually have survived after all. If there is a sequel doubtless we will discover. Less noticed by the fans is the title *Ex Machina*. Some readers may be familiar with the Latin tag *deus ex machina*, literally 'God from a machine'. In Ancient Greece the plots of plays could sometimes become so entangled that the directors had to swing in a god (using a wooden machine) to resolve them. In the modern world *deus ex machina* has become a tag identifying a particularly poor argument that, say, uses God inappropriately to resolve a problem. Perhaps this was in Garland's mind. After all, at the outset there is an observation by the visitor that the scientist has been 'playing God' in creating this humanoid robot. Perhaps this scientist/god had neglected to give his artefact a moral sense.

This speculation apart, we probably don't need science fiction to remind us that some humanoids appear to be devoid of a moral sense. Simon Sebag Montefiore's *Stalin: The court of the Red Tsar* offers a deeply shocking example from real life, as its blurb suggests: 'In this history of Stalin's imperial court, the fear and betrayal, privilege and debauchery, family life and murderous brutality are brought blazingly to life.'[1] Stalin's murderous brutality spread outwards from his own family and close colleagues to millions of his own people. Anyone offering criticism, political opposition or simply non-compliance was threatened with extinction. Indeed, Stalin soon learned that extinction was the most effective way to end dissent. He seemed to be at least as devoid of moral compunction as *Ex Machina*'s humanoid robot.

The Mafia contract killer Richard Kuklinski (1935–2006) is another example of someone seemingly devoid of moral compunction. After a quarter of a century of contract killing he was eventually convicted of five murders and imprisoned for life but not executed. While he was serving his whole-life sentence he was able to give extensive interviews to journalists and criminologists. In these he confessed to the murder of more than a hundred other people, including a policeman. He claimed to have proved his worth initially to the Mafia by calmly killing an innocent pedestrian when ordered to do so by a Mafia boss. He apparently took particular pride in devising different methods of torturing and murdering his victims (including the use of a crossbow to kill a stranger simply to test out its effectiveness). He was so prolific a murderer – both for the Mafia and for his own satisfaction (often just to settle petty personal grudges) – and so morally unconcerned about his actions that he inspired a film and voyeuristic book about his life based upon hours of his prison interviews. How could he have been so morally indifferent about his monstrous actions?

John Webster, one of the first British soldiers to witness the horrors of the Belsen concentration camp, died recently aged 93. His *Times* obituary recalled:

> Noticing a group of white buildings through the trees that, as he put it 'looked not quite right', he turned off down a track to investigate . . . He found an empty pit 25 yards long and nine feet deep, then another, a few yards farther on, filled with skeletal bones. Beyond the pits were the first group of emaciated survivors, still and silent in their blue and white striped pyjamas or rags of civilian clothes, looking at him with unseeing eyes, many of them too traumatised to show any joy that their incarceration was over . . . Asked in old age about his reaction to entering Belsen in 1945, he replied: 'To see human beings reduced to this state, and to think that other human beings had done this to them, well, I still try to make sense of it. What did it mean? You can't explain the inexplicable.'[2]

For quite a while in mid-twentieth-century philosophy it was fashionable to argue that morality at base is simply about personal taste, feelings or preferences. On this understanding there is nothing that is objectively good or bad. There are just some things that I feel to be good or prefer or that are to my taste and other things that are not. But are these three egregious examples really just a matter of personal distaste? Obviously I would prefer them not to have happened. And they do give me (and doubtless you as well) a very nasty feeling. But is that enough?

Of course there *are* some trivial things that we tend to get morally indignant about. Hairstyles or table manners are good examples. They differ very widely across time and across different cultures, yet feelings about them are often very strong. Moving swiftly on one occasion from China to South Korea and then to Japan, I discovered that eating rice with chopsticks was deeply problematic. The length and style of the chopsticks differed markedly from one country to the next, as did the table manners expected. Having longer legs than most of the local people and being unused to sitting cross-legged on the floor I found it very difficult to deliver any rice to my mouth using these varying chopsticks. In China it appeared to be acceptable to pick up your rice bowl and scoop its contents into your mouth. I could do *that*. However, before attempting to do the same in South Korea, I asked my host if this was acceptable. He told me politely that it was extremely rude. So uncrossing my legs and leaning forward instead I could just about eat the rice, but unfortunately the waitress tripped over my feet sticking out from the other side of the table. My witless table manners left a very poor impression.

The length of men's hair can also evoke strong feelings of distaste, sometimes because it is too long and sometimes because it is too short. Long hair mimicking fashionable seventeenth-century wigs can now be deemed to be louche. Short haircuts that were *de rigueur* in the 1940s may now appear too aggressive. Fashions change but moral indignation endures. Does that apply to all of morality?

Are we to say the same about our moral reactions to Stalin, Kuklinski and the perpetrators of the Belsen concentration camp? Is our moral indignation against them just the product of changeable cultural taste? Given the right circumstances, might we one day conclude that their actions are morally acceptable?

I doubt if many would reach this conclusion. There does seem to be something that is deeply and *objectively* evil about such actions. Sentient human beings should know – unless their minds have been severely damaged – that such murderous actions can never be morally justified. There has been much speculation about Kuklinski's brain or mental health. As just mentioned he appeared to express little or no moral remorse about his grotesque actions. Perhaps he had a damaged genetic inheritance, a cerebral injury, an appalling upbringing, or perhaps he just gradually slipped into insentient behaviour (apparently a number of serial killers start, as he did, by torturing animals). Yet such explanations can soon become excuses and many of us may feel that deep in his mind he *must* still have known that his murderous actions were fundamentally immoral. After all, unlike the humanoid robot in *Ex Machina*, he was unambiguously a human being.

On this basis we might conclude that some human actions really are evil – that is, that they are objectively wrong. There does seem to be a trend in recent philosophy in this direction, concluding that the moral relativism adopted so often in the mid-twentieth century was misleading. It's a slender basis for answering the question 'Why be good?' but it is still a significant one. If some things are deemed to be objectively evil, then it may be reasonable to conclude that other things are objectively good. And surely it is then reasonable to conclude that we should pursue the good and eschew what is evil.

Or is it?

2

Because if I scratch your back you will scratch mine

We left our Parador Hotel before daybreak to drive 40 minutes to the extraordinary small town of El Rocio deep in southern Spain. For much of the year El Rocio is a ghost town waiting for the annual surge of one million pilgrims and 28,000 horses to celebrate the Feast of Pentecost. Fortunately for us Pentecost was still months away. Meanwhile El Rocio is the gateway for accompanied trips around the Doñana National Park, the extensive protected swampland where the European wild lynx still lives. We saw plenty of birds, deer and wild boar, but no lynx. Just the fresh and unmistakable tracks in the sand of a lone adult lynx. They are solitary, nocturnal animals that hide in thick bushes during daylight. Quite different from the pack of lionesses that used the shadow of our vehicle in South Africa as cover while they stalked prey in full daylight, or dozed together in the open, while we drove through their midst, when it grew too hot.

The lone lynx and the cooperative lioness offer contrasting metaphors for human behaviour in the modern world. Sometimes we picture people today as autonomous individuals each doing their own thing, obsessed by self-interest, reading their iPhones as they walk and with earphones blocking out sound from the outside world, or sitting for hours in front of a computer screen (as I am doing now). The selfish gene or the free spirit – as you wish. The lynx.

At other times we picture people today and in the past as essentially social animals. We live, work, eat and commute together within vast cities, we have different functions that meld together, we interact and communicate with each other endlessly, and we rely upon each other from birth to the grave. The dependent cooperative being. The lioness.

The lynx and the lioness represent two very different approaches to ethics today: one concerned with the individual and the other with the group. Both have something important to say but there is also a clear tension between them. Taking my own area of medical ethics, the difference is as follows:

The lynx is the patient taken on her own as an individual. She needs to be treated with respect and allowed to make autonomous decisions about any medical interventions that are offered to her. Unless there is clear evidence to the contrary, she must be treated as a competent individual who can make up her own mind about what treatment is in her best interest. She must be given adequate information about what choices of treatment she has and what their various consequences might be and, if she says 'no' to any or all of them, then that treatment must not be given to her. She cannot require a particular treatment against the judgement of her doctor, but she can refuse even life-sustaining treatment and that refusal is then binding upon the doctor. She is also entitled to confidentiality about her medical condition. Assumed competence, informed consent, the right to refuse and confidentiality are all essential parts of patient autonomy. In modern medical ethics and law patient autonomy is a cornerstone.

Some critics have argued that patient autonomy is a misguided and selfish notion. We should trust our doctors and be less lynx-like as patients. The solitary patient is given an unrealistic burden of decision-making about areas well beyond her competence and the role of, say, her family is ignored. I could not agree less. I regard patient autonomy as a real moral gain and would have little respect for my doctor if she ignored it. I do expect to have adequate information about the medical choices that I have and to be fully involved in medical decisions that are made about me. Only in that way can I feel properly responsible for my own health. So I can agree with the lynx.

The lioness starts from a different position. Her behaviour suggests that there are huge benefits to be had from cooperating fully with other lionesses. Lionesses hunt strategically together more effectively than they might on their own, and with several pairs of eyes can more easily spot potential prey as well as dangers. They care for their young together who, in turn, are protected by their resident father from their main predator, namely another male lion. Or, to express this in terms of medical ethics, public health (the most basic of all medical interventions) depends upon cooperation to produce healthy drinking water and a sanitary environment in which all can live. Herd immunity is enhanced by public vaccination programmes that may or may not benefit particular individuals but result in an overall benefit to the community at large. Decisions about the allocation of scarce medical resources (such as hearts for transplantation or highly expensive cancer drugs) need to consider whole populations rather than just the autonomous requests of individuals.

There is an obvious tension between lynx-like and lioness-like approaches. A patient with a terminal and otherwise untreatable heart condition and her family may be desperate for a transplant, but the transplant team may decide that some other patient should be given priority. Parents who are fearful of possible side effects from a vaccination may decide not to have their child vaccinated and to rely instead upon local herd immunity. Yet if enough parents in the same area reach the same conclusion this herd immunity may be badly compromised. Apparently autonomous patient decisions may have unexpected, dire consequences for other people.

Even the solitary lynx is dependent upon the very people that it shuns and by whom it was once hunted. As you travel through the Doñana you see uprooted trees laid side by side by the wardens. The trees themselves are eucalyptus, a non-native species introduced into Andalucia from Australia, that are now considered to be inappropriate within a conservation area. However, their husks provide protection for rabbits, the main source of food for the protected lynx. The lynx may be solitary and secretive but it too is dependent upon others for its survival.

There is now a growing awareness of interdependence and of the importance of cooperation among environmentalists, evolutionists and others working in a variety of areas. Our bodies themselves contain genes, chromosomes and cells that cooperate. Our social lives and societies at large are constructed around cooperation. In a globalized world, countries such as North Korea have to go to considerable lengths not to cooperate with other countries and even North Korea finally cooperates (up to a point) with China. Human infectious diseases cross territorial boundaries and require international cooperation if they are to be countered effectively. Carbon emissions, AIDS and antibiotic resistance are all manifestly global problems that also require global cooperation. Even in the supposedly individualistic modern world we have need for the lioness as well as the lynx. The instinctive behaviour of swarms of birds, fish and even ants suggests as much. By swarming together they provide mutual protection in an otherwise hostile environment. And ants have discovered that suicidal attacks by some of their members tend to deter aggressors.

The aphorism 'you scratch my back and I will scratch yours' is a minimal way of expressing the ethical approach here. We should be good to others so that they might be good to us. Or to express this negatively, if we do evil to others we might well expect them to do evil to us. Every tyrant such as Stalin knows this only too well. Once he is known to eliminate opponents, he must go to great lengths to ensure that opponents do not succeed in eliminating him first. In other words, those who live by the sword must expect to die by the sword.

Understood in this way, the answer to our question 'Why be good?' is simply enlightened self-interest: it is basically in our self-interest to be good.

Some believe that that is a sufficient answer and have even devised elaborate (and mathematically complex) game theories to prove it. Ethics finally boils down to self-interest. In the business world this has sometimes been championed. If a business is widely thought to be run on an ethical basis, then it is likely to be trusted by the general public. As a result people will invest in it and have confidence in its products. Conversely, if an investment firm, say, is suspected of being based upon a so-called Ponzi scheme (in which investors are paid not with genuine returns on their money but simply with other people's money that is supposed instead to be invested), it is unlikely that people will continue to invest in it. So being seen to be ethical becomes simply a feature of prudence rather than ethics.

Unfortunately there is a flaw in this business example. The trusted business has only to be *seen* by the public to be ethical. Some of the most successful Ponzi schemes have been run by people who were thoroughly trusted by others despite being unmasked later as being deeply corrupt. It is possible that *the* most successful Ponzi schemes are still being run by deeply corrupt but exceedingly persuasive people who have cunningly avoided detection and never been unmasked. The crucial factor here is public perception or trust, not personal honesty as such. A public figure who is privately honest but is thought to be corrupt by the wider public (or who simply looks shifty) would, on this basis, make a very poor head of any investment scheme.

So we reach the strange conclusion that our question should be 'Why be *thought* to be good?' and not 'Why be good?' We have reached a clear conclusion, but only by changing the question.

Let's go back to the original question. A better answer might be: we should be good because cooperation is good.

But that answer sides too strongly with the lionesses. Lionesses do cooperate for their own good but not necessarily for the benefit of everything around them. That is not, of course, their fault. They are, after all, lionesses. With elephants (another cooperative species) this is even more problematic. A herd of roaming elephants tends to leave a trail of ecological devastation behind it. But we are humans and, as many of us increasingly believe, we have responsibilities for the wider environment, including that of the lionesses and elephants. We are also humans that sometimes cooperate for evil purposes. Gang rape or criminal fraternities are obvious examples.

And, besides that, lynx-like personal autonomy is also important to many of us. But how far do you take that autonomy? The so-called Golden Rule offers one widely held path: do to others as you would want them to do to you. Or, to express this negatively: do not do to others as you would not want them to do to you.

The Golden Rule requires more than simple cooperation. In its positive form it requires us to respect other people in the same way that we respect ourselves. And that, of course, can be very demanding. I will come back to that in the final chapter. For the moment, though, it is worth noting some of the problems with the Golden Rule.

Using the Golden Rule I confess that I would make a very poor dentist or general medical practitioner. I make my own dentist flinch because I would rather put up with some sharp temporary pain than have an injection that numbs my jaw for hours. If I were a dentist most of my patients would be horrified to be treated as I would want to be treated myself. Again, with my GP I would rather have clear factual information about possible treatments and their consequences than empathy. In contrast, many other patients regard a good 'bedside manner', as it is quaintly termed, to be an essential quality for any clinical doctor. My oddities apart, we do differ from each other about how we want to be treated, so our expectations of treatment may not match those of others.

Another problem lies in the very foundation of the Golden Rule. As will be seen later the Golden Rule is widely held across different cultures and religious traditions. Nevertheless, however widespread, cultures and religious traditions may arguably be misguided. So on what is it based? Most obviously it might be based once again upon self-interest. Treating others as I would want to be treated myself seems to ensure that I, in turn, will be treated fairly by others. Or, to put that negatively, if I don't treat people properly I can hardly be surprised if they, in turn, don't treat me properly. Some quite complex philosophical explanations have been based upon this seemingly simple premise, dependent as it is upon self-interest.

Yet manipulative people might soon conclude that it is not in their interest to treat others fairly, it is only in *their* interest to be treated fairly by others. The best of all possible worlds for them (strictly in terms of self-interest) would be for them to receive much better treatment from others than they are prepared to give out themselves. That is what many manipulative people tend to seek. It is also what greedy people tend to seek. Giving an equal part of a cake to everyone will never satisfy the seriously greedy. They want to have more cake than everyone else. And, as greedy people, it is in their self-interest to ensure that by one means or another this happens.

Another problem is more high-minded than this. Altruists may want to give other people better treatment than they get themselves. Suppose I really had decided to become a GP (I come from a family of doctors), I hope that I would have had the moral sensitivity to treat my patients with empathy despite not particularly requiring it for myself. More importantly, moral heroes (as we shall see in the next chapter) go considerably beyond self-interest and a narrow reading of the Golden Rule. For them it is not a question of treating others as they would want to be treated themselves. They are prepared to treat others even better than they treat themselves. A narrow reading of the Golden Rule is not for them.

The upshot of all of this is that self-interest, or better mutual self-interest, does offer a rational basis for answering the question 'Why be good?' But it does not extend very far and it faces some fairly obvious problems. And it gives quite a weak answer to the issue raised in the final paragraph of the last chapter:

If some things are deemed to be objectively evil, then it may be reasonable to conclude that other things are objectively good. And surely it is then reasonable to conclude that we should pursue the good and eschew what is evil.

Arguments based simply upon mutual self-interest tend to elide 'evil' with 'what is not in our self-interest'. The sort of evils depicted in the previous chapter might well be considered not to be in the self-interest of most people (Stalin, Kuklinski and their kindred spirits apart). Nevertheless, many of us might want to say something rather stronger about monstrous evil than that.

Is there a better basis? The next chapter will look at duty and will ask whether or not we have a duty to be good and to oppose what is evil.

3

Because it is our duty

In July 1982 a Scottish van driver, Robert Black, raped and murdered an 11-year-old schoolgirl, Susie Maxwell. He had snatched her in full daylight near Coldstream Bridge between England and Scotland. As I write he has just died in prison aged 69, having been convicted of the murder of four girls aged 5 to 11 (three of whom he raped) and suspected of many more child-killings. Susie's disappearance was national news until her body was found dumped 250 miles away. There was then a nationwide search for the person who had committed this most heinous of crimes, torturing and murdering a child for his own sexual satisfaction. He was eventually caught eight years later in the act of kidnapping another girl at Stow in the Scottish Borders. A vigilant member of the public spotted a seeming abduction, noted the number-plate of the van and immediately phoned the police. A local policeman stopped the van as it returned to the village and found a girl bound and taped in the back of Black's van. The girl he discovered, thankfully still alive, was his own daughter.

The case was deeply shocking for many, many people, but for us as a family it was personal. We lived in a neighbouring small village, had children of the same age and travelling on the same school bus, and Susie Maxwell's family was well known within the community. Until it became clear that this child-killer was operating across the country, adult males in the local community all came under suspicion and those of us with young children became fearful for their safety. A strong sense of duty was felt by many of us. The men (even some of the local GPs) had a duty to supply the police with saliva swabs. Families had a duty to warn their children without traumatizing them. The police had a duty to do everything that they could to find the child-killer. The local press had a duty to report the case without becoming prurient (Susie Maxwell's poor mother was herself a journalist). The churches had a duty to pray for her and for her family. The memories of this shocking event and the dutiful and heart-felt response of the local community are still very vivid for us.

A sense of duty is not unambiguous. Notoriously many prisoners loathe child-killers. On at least two occasions a fellow prisoner felt it was his duty to murder Robert Black and attempted to act upon this misguided sense of duty. A duty for revenge can be strongly felt. Black must have had a miserable and traumatic 34 years in prison. He was also facing the prospect of another trial for murder just before he died. Whatever sexual pleasure he had derived from his profoundly dysfunctional actions, he must have experienced years of violent hatred from other prisoners and perhaps from some prison staff as well. He had deeply offended family people everywhere, prisoners and non-prisoners alike.

Although a sense of duty can sometimes be misguided – and for this reason it must not bypass critical inspection – it does still represent a stronger moral position than an approach based solely upon calculated self-interest. A sense of duty has an element of moral passion that is often missing from calculated self-interest. This is especially important when considering the motives of those who act courageously against their own narrow self-interest but for the good of others. Noel Chavasse offers an extraordinary and well-documented example of this.

Noel Chavasse was a First World War doctor who was one of only three people ever to have been awarded two Victoria Crosses (a Victoria Cross and bar). Both medals for exceptional gallantry within war were awarded to him for repeatedly rescuing wounded soldiers while being under fire and wounded himself. The second was awarded posthumously after he died from his wounds. Given all that we now know about the ghastly trench warfare at the time, his actions are almost unimaginable. *The London Gazette* (September 1917) captured something of his extraordinary courage leading up to his death in August 1917:

> Early in the action he was severely wounded in the head while carrying a wounded man to his dressing station. He refused to leave his post and for two days not only continued to attend the cases brought to his first aid post, but repeatedly and under heavy fire went out to the firing line with stretcher parties to search for the wounded and dressed those lying out. During these searches he found a number of badly wounded men in the open and assisted to carry them in over heavy and difficult ground.

He was practically without food during this period, worn with fatigue and faint from his wounds. By his extraordinary energy and inspiring example he was instrumental in succouring many men who must otherwise have succumbed under the bad weather conditions. On the morning of August 2nd he was again wounded seriously by a shell and died in hospital on August 4th.

Thanks to his family letters and the research of Selwyn Gummer we know quite a bit about what motivated Noel Chavasse. He was brought up in an intensely evangelical family: his father was Principal of Wycliffe Hall and then Bishop of Liverpool and the family held daily prayers together. He was extremely close to his identical twin brother (who eventually became Bishop of Rochester) and had twin sisters and two other brothers. All four of the brothers served in the First World War but only one (who, like Noel, was killed in the war) was a combatant. His twin was a chaplain and he and the other brother were medics, and all three of them were awarded a Military Cross in addition to his own Victoria Crosses. A strong sense of duty and religious conviction ran through the whole family. While he was a medical student he taught in a Sunday School and 'found time in the midst of his studies to start a Bible Class in the industrial school which he conducted up to the outbreak of war; he held twice a week a Boys' Union for prayer and Bible reading'.[3] In later life his fiancée (and cousin):

> remembered him as a profoundly devout person. His faith was the first thing in his life; once he had talked to her of taking orders and of becoming a medical missionary when the horror of war was passed. She for her part

20

welcomed this prospect. His interest in the youth work he had undertaken in Liverpool before the war was so great that he could never have been satisfied with ministering only to the physical needs of men and women. He would have to have become in some way a physician of the soul.[4]

In his final note to his fiancée after his fatal wound he wrote simply: 'Duty called and duty must be obeyed'.[5]

A sense of duty is difficult to understand or justify in purely rational terms. Most famously it has been defined as acting on the maxim that we would wish our behaviour to become a universal law. Expressed in these terms it has obvious affinity with the Golden Rule and, as a result, shares some of its weaknesses when viewed in purely rational terms. Or to express this differently, both the Golden Rule and this concept of duty require an act of faith on our part – a basic faith that we really should treat other people fairly and not exploit them for our own benefit. The determinedly self-centred are likely to have little truck with either the Golden Rule or this understanding of duty. Unfortunately this can become very circular: this understanding of duty is designed to give us a rational account that does not depend upon faith, but in reality, like the Golden Rule, it does require an act of faith.

Yet, whether we can justify it rationally or not, most of us do have a sense of duty especially towards our children (which makes Robert Black's actions so abhorrent to us). Most of us who have heterosexual intercourse while we are still fertile know that it can result in a child being born. Unless the woman has a miscarriage or abortion, most of us then feel a sense of duty towards the child once it is born. Most parents, thankfully, go to great lengths to ensure that their children are loved, cared for, educated and brought up to behave properly to other people. And we think little of parents who feel no sense of duty to do all of this and are deeply sorry for their children.

'Ah,' says the critic: 'This is just mother nature.' Well, up to a point. Mammals do characteristically nurture their young, as do most birds but few reptiles or fish. However, among mammals it is quite varied about whether it is just the mother or both the mother and father who do this nurturing. In most human societies it is expected that both parents will have a role in nurturing the young, extending over many years. 'Yes,' the critic responds: 'Surely this is also a function of mother nature given that it takes years for the brain to develop.' But there is a crucial difference to note here. Humans can think and they can communicate their thoughts to other human beings. And because they can think and talk they can (as we know only too well) talk themselves out of bringing up their own children. Equally (and more usually) they can be persuaded through thought and language that it is their duty to bring up their own children. Duty then becomes not simply an instinct of nature but a conscious sense of moral imperative. This in turn convinces most of us that spending time to bring up our children well is indeed the right thing to do and that not even attempting to do this would be wrong.

Many people also have had a sense of duty to defend their country, however reluctantly, in a time of warfare. After the devastations of the First World War it was widely expected in the 1930s that large sections of the British population would refuse to be enlisted if there was ever another war. This expectation was soon disproved in 1939 with the threat of Nazi aggression and possible invasion. As a one-time pacifist in my youth I can well understand those few who were conscientious objectors. Yet it is worth noting that they too often expressed a strong sense of duty, if only a duty to witness against warfare, and that many of them found other non-military ways of serving their country during the war.

In addition, many of us have a sense of duty to pay taxes and to be honest and responsible citizens. Few exactly admire tax-dodgers and citizens who are dishonest and/or irresponsible. Civil society depends upon most of us having such a sense of duty towards our fellow citizens and soon disintegrates (as in civil wars) when such a sense of duty is lost. The rule of law within pluralistic democracies depends upon most citizens having such a sense of civil duty.

The ecological movement also depends upon a sense of duty. We increasingly believe that we have a duty to care for our planet that goes well beyond our own personal benefit. Climate change might even seem attractive to people on a cold winter's day if they were concerned solely with own comfort. Yet slowly we are beginning to realize that we need to take action to curtail our own short-term consumption of natural resources and carbon emissions in order to benefit future generations of humans and wildlife.

However, none of this matches the extraordinary sense of duty of someone like Noel Chavasse. To this we might add moral heroes such as President Nelson Mandela, the Dalai Lama or Archbishop Desmond Tutu, all of whom acted long for others well beyond their own self-interest. Doubtless each of them enjoyed some of the international praise they received and drew some personal satisfaction from that. Yet there are much easier and less dangerous ways of gaining such praise (as many a celebrity will know). By risking their lives and personal welfare each demonstrated a passionate sense of duty well beyond mutual self-interest.

Each of these moral heroes – with the possible exception of Nelson Mandela, but that is much disputed – was also strongly religious. So it is tempting at this point in my argument to fly in the Ancient Greek gods from the edge of the stage that gave rise to the tag *deus ex machina* (noted in the first chapter). All is then resolved. We need religion to uphold a passionate and heroic sense of moral duty in society. Morality based solely upon rational principles is just too weak to nourish a heroic sense of duty in times of danger.

However, I wish to avoid this conclusion for two very obvious reasons:

The first has already been noted: I want all people to have a sense of morality whether they have a sense of religious faith or not. I see no merit in claiming that only religious people can have a proper sense of morality.

The second is more sinister: in the twenty-first century we have become acutely aware that religious passion can sometimes become deeply destructive. After 9/11 and 7/7 and numerous atrocities committed by religious fundamentalists since, how could we not be so aware? The very phrase 'God is good' to be used in the heading of the next chapter is too close to the war-cry in Arabic of would-be suicide bombers that 'God is great' – that is, of people who believe that acts of atrocity upon civilians are responses to commands by God. It is difficult to think of an understanding of God that is further from the faith of most practising Jews, Christians and Muslims in Western society. Yet those of us who are religious are now in danger of simply being lumped together with these violent fundamentalists in the present along with our violent counterparts, such as the Crusaders, in the distant past.

Our critics have astonishing short cultural memories. The deeply anti-religious Stalin has already been mentioned, but the equally anti-religious Pol Pot and Mao Zedong might also be recalled – each directly responsible for millions of deaths of their own citizens in the twentieth century. Neither secular nor religious passion has clean hands. We need to sift carefully and not to over-claim.

Given such careful sifting and without over-claiming, does belief in a loving God give Jews, Christians and Muslims at least a steer in responding to the question 'Why be good'?

4

Because God is good

Ancient Greek philosophers wrestled with a dilemma that ran like this: is an act good because God says that it is so, or does God say that it is so because it is good?

Now if we answer that an act is indeed good because God says that it is so, then that appears to make goodness an arbitrary whim of God. It is a bit like double yellow lines on the side of roads to prevent people parking. There is nothing about double yellow lines that tells foreigners that they have anything to do with parking, let alone that parking on them is forbidden. In one Nordic country, as a foreigner myself, I hired a car and bought tickets in advance for parking in blue zones. I used them to do just that but discovered later that they only worked in pale blue parking zones, not in navy blue parking zones. The residents must have thought that I was an idiot. It never occurred to me that their parking authorities would make such a subtle distinction. In any case I found it difficult to understand the Nordic English in which the instructions were written. National regulations about parking can be highly whimsical. Perhaps that would be true of goodness too if it simply depended upon the whim of God.

On the other hand, if we answer that God says that an act is good because it is so, we also have a problem. God and goodness appear to be separate entities, with God being subject to goodness. Goodness even appears to be a higher power than God. So God does not appear to be the creator of everything (as Jews, Christians and Muslims all claim). God, on this understanding, did not create goodness, but rather goodness shaped God.

I do not want to spend the rest of the chapter on this dilemma (whole books have been written about it). Philosophers who believe in God usually opt for a version of the first answer but tweak it. So goodness becomes not a whimsical command of God but an essential feature of God's character. God being God cannot be anything other than good. Ultimate goodness and God are finally one and the same, just as God and ultimate love are finally one and the same. We are stretching language here but that, I believe, is unavoidable when we talk about God. If we reduce God simply to human terms we are not really talking about God at all. We might also recall that God, properly understood, is outside of time. So it makes no sense, for example, to ask: which came first, God or goodness? Both God and goodness are eternal.

Whether or not you find this answer satisfactory, it is worth noting that the atheist also has a problem. By denying the existence of God the atheist cannot ground morality in a *created* universe. For the atheist the universe is fortuitous, not created, and it is by no means clear why the structure of a fortuitous universe should give us any clues at all about moral goodness. Some moral philosophers, for example, have tried to use a theory of evolution to bolster morality. The features of an evolving universe for them can generate moral laws about protecting the environment and cooperating with each other (back to lionesses again). I am committed to evolutionary theory myself, but I cannot see why it gives a satisfactory answer to my question 'Why be good?' After all, human beings spend quite a bit of energy trying to counteract evolutionary trends by, say, preserving animal and plant species that would otherwise become extinct. Much of modern medicine is also aimed at countering evolutionary trends, allowing those who would not otherwise survive to do so and to have children. In addition, as we have already seen, cooperation is not always virtuous. Finally, I am particularly puzzled by those atheists who insist that evolution is 'a blind force' yet seek to derive moral laws from it.

So what exactly does a belief in God add to being morally good? It would take another book to answer this question properly, but it is worth sketching three distinctive ways in which the Abrahamic faiths (Judaism, Islam and Christianity) can add something important for those of us who do believe in God. Specifically Judaism addresses the relationship between God's faithfulness to us even in times of persecution and our proper moral response to each other and to God. Islam, especially in its understanding of hospitality towards strangers, has an important emphasis upon the compassion of God and our moral duty to others in need. And Christianity has a radical requirement for us to love those who hate us, just as God loves each one of us however vile we become. Each of these is an emphasis and not an exclusive possession of any single faith tradition. Yet, for those who believe in God, each also adds something significant to a purely secular understanding of morality. Just as importantly these Abrahamic faith traditions also offer guidance, ritual practices and examples to nurture human goodness.

In Judaism God's faithfulness is enshrined in the covenants first with Noah and then with Abraham. I was brought up in Golders Green and had many Jewish friends at school. Being naturally religious I was delighted when they invited me to their special festivals. On one occasion I went to a friend's bar mitzvah, the special coming-of-age ceremony for teenage boys in a synagogue. For this my friend had to learn to recite a passage of Hebrew from the Bible in public (which I think he did entirely from memory and not by reading the Hebrew text). Later I also went to his wedding in a grand Orthodox Synagogue in central London. However, for me, the most privileged occasion was taking part in a Passover meal with his family. The youngsters were all given four small glasses of watered-down wine, together with unleavened bread and bitter herbs, as a senior member of the family recited the story of the Passover from the Hebrew Bible. Throughout the ceremony there was a strong sense of family in the faithful presence of God.

Writing about the Passover, my favourite Jewish writer, Rabbi (now Lord) Jonathan Sacks, retells the biblical story of the Israelites being turned into slaves under a tyrannical Egyptian pharaoh and their children being drowned in the Nile:

Slavery began to darken into genocide. And then something happened, something that we have remembered
ever since. An Israelite who by chance had been brought
up as an Egyptian saw what was happening to his people . . .
The man was Moses, and although his mission had many
setbacks and disappointed hopes, eventually he led the
Israelites to freedom and to the brink of the promised
land. There the story might have ended, were it not that
from the very outset the Bible seems to sense that the
journey from slavery to freedom is one we need to travel
in every generation. So we are commanded to gather
together every year at this time and tell the story of what
it was like to be a slave and what it felt like to go free.
Not just tell the story, but act it out too . . . We tell the
story in such a way that each of us feels as if we have
lived through persecution and come out the other side
as free human beings – as if history had been lifted off
the page to become recent memory. That is how we
cherish freedom.[6]

Freedom under God is still recalled at the Passover meal
re-enacted for generation after generation. For the Jewish
family in Golders Green this must have been particularly poignant in the 1950s. They were not an especially
devout family for the rest of the year, but Passover was
very special and a deep reminder of family members who
had been murdered in Nazi Europe.

Whenever I take a wedding in church I always say
three things. The first is that the couple and their
family have chosen to come to a beautiful place of wor-
ship, which has hosted many such weddings over the
years, *and* to celebrate this wedding in the presence of
God. The second is that they have chosen to make their

vows not just to each other *but also* to God. And the third
is to invite those of us who are married, or about to
be married, to repeat these vows silently to each other
and to God. In other words, this is an explicitly religious
ceremony that deepens the significance of what we are
all doing together in the presence of God. Of course the
secular side of marriage is important too and the public
signing of the registers at the end of a Church of England
wedding is a reminder of this. But a church wedding for
people of faith adds an extra depth. Perhaps that is what
my otherwise secular Jewish family felt at Passover after
the horrors of the Jewish holocaust.

If Rabbi Jonathan Sacks is my favourite Jewish writer,
Professor Mona Siddiqui is my favourite Muslim writer.
Like Sacks she writes as both a scholar and practising
person of faith who also can relate knowledgeably and
eirenically to the other Abrahamic faith traditions and to
wider secular Western culture. Her recent book *Hospitality
and Islam: Welcoming in God's name* offers a rich account
of hospitality in Islamic and Christian history contrasted
sympathetically with secular writings on hospitality. She
argues that Islamic (and Christian) understandings of
hospitality are deepened and enriched by a belief in God:

> In the Qur'an . . . hospitality is first and foremost a duty
> towards others, and a way of living in which we are
> constantly reminded of human diversity. There are over-
> lapping discourses on food as a blessing to be shared with
> others and food as a means of enjoying the company
> of others. There are multiple commandments to give
> charity and shelter, to feed others, to look after widows,
> neighbours, travellers and orphans. We must give and be

> generous because this is how God is and God's giving knows no limits. Hospitality is not necessarily premised on pleasure, and yet pleasure enhances the experience of doing hospitality.[7]

She is well aware that critics of Islam have argued, at least since medieval times, that Muslims are too pre-occupied with physical/sensuous rewards in the next life in return for good works (including hospitality and charitable giving) done in this life. However, she maintains that this rests upon a highly superficial view of Islam and of the Qur'an in particular. The latter, she points out, uses separate Arabic words to differentiate between charitable giving that is a required duty (one of the five pillars of Islam) and charitable giving that goes beyond duty. And the fundamental premise of all good work is compassion. It is God's compassion to us that should inspire us to be compassionate to each other. Indeed, every chapter but one in the Qur'an begins with the invocation: 'In the name of God, the Lord of Mercy/Compassion, the Giver of Mercy/Compassion':

> It is to God we turn for all our needs, for God is always the ultimate refuge. If the structural context implicit in the devotional vocabulary of Christianity is different from that of Islam, the practical obligation to show care and hospitality remains the same. I would contend that offering hospitality [especially to the stranger] as a way of imitating the divine, as well as being obedient to God, is embedded in the rich vocabulary of charity, generosity, mercy and compassion which permeates the entire Qur'an.[8]

At a time of deep international concern about the European refugee crisis this reminder is especially important. Hospitality to the stranger in need has long been a strong moral imperative within Judaism, Christianity and Islam even if their adherents have sometimes ignored it. This imperative is not simply based upon feeling sorry for the dislocated and needy (although that is important). It derives from a belief about God's prior compassion for us and from faith that we do not live in a fortuitous universe but in a universe created through love and compassion.

Christianity shares the Golden Rule in one form or another with Judaism and Islam (do/don't do to others as you would want/not want them to do to you). Some have also traced versions of the Golden Rule in Buddhism, Hinduism and Confucianism. We have already seen some problems with the Golden Rule if it is handled too bluntly. However, if it is interpreted generously it can be an important maxim for moral living. Treating other people as compassionately as most of us would want to be treated ourselves does appear to be a morally virtuous position to take. Even though moral heroes go much further than this (as we have already seen), mutual compassion, if it really were followed by all, would surely result in a morally better world.

But the problem in the previous sentence is the clause 'if it really were followed by all'. Sadly we know that that is not going to happen. Some people seem incapable of being compassionate to others, especially to those they have some grudge against. Richard Kuklinski was not alone in bearing grudges.

33

It is at this point that Jesus in the Gospels was much more demanding to his followers. In the Sermon on the Mount in St Matthew's Gospel he is reported as saying:

> You have heard that it was said, 'You shall love your neighbour and hate your enemy.' But I say to you, love your enemies and pray for those who persecute you.[9]

And in St Luke's Gospel when Jesus was asked, 'Who is my neighbour?' he replied by telling the parable of the Good Samaritan. The Israelites and the Samaritans were traditional enemies but in this parable it is the Samaritan and not the passing Israelites who comes to the rescue of the person left half dead by robbers on the roadside. So neighbour-love is ascribed to a traditional enemy and prayer is required for one's own persecutors. This is an ethic indeed for those moral heroes mentioned earlier, such as Nelson Mandela, Desmond Tutu and the Dalai Lama.

I suspect that Mona Siddiqui and Jonathan Sacks might also agree with this position. A radical belief in God really does seem to push us further than most of us might otherwise want. If God really does love flawed human beings like me and you, then the least we can do is try to love other people regardless of what they do or say to us. This is no longer mutual love, let alone mutual self-interest. It is love that may never be requited. Self-giving love. Demanding love. Love beyond any glow of self-satisfaction. Practising Christians celebrate this love shown by Jesus every time that we share the Eucharist together. If only we really could also demonstrate such love in our lives.

Perhaps, even in a pluralistic and sometimes secular world, Abrahamic faith traditions do have something important to add in response to the question 'Why be good?' What these three faith traditions add may well challenge us deeply and push us beyond our comfort zone. That, I believe, is one of the functions of faith. But it also offers hope that, with the grace of God, we really could live morally better lives. Jews, Christians and Muslims surely should try to do this together.

Jonathan Sacks ends his latest book *Not in God's Name: Confronting religious violence*, as I too will end, with a passionate plea to Jews, Christians and Muslims to recover together a purer form of faith:

> We need to recover the absolute values that make Abrahamic monotheism the humanising force it has been at its best: the sanctity of life, the dignity of the individual, the twin imperatives of justice and compassion, the moral responsibility of the rich for the poor, the commands to love the neighbour and stranger, the insistence on peaceful means of conflict resolution and respectful listening to the other side of a case, forgiving the injuries of the past and focusing instead on building a future in which the children of the world, of all colours, faith and races, can live together in grace and peace. These are the ideals on which Jews, Christians and Muslims can converge, widening their embrace to include those of other faiths and none.[10]

Notes

1 Simon Sebag Montefiore, *Stalin: The court of the Red Tsar*, London: Phoenix Orion paperback, 2014 (first published by Weidenfeld & Nicolson: London, 2003).

2 *The Times*, 11 January 2016, p. 41.

3 Selwyn Gummer, *The Chavasse Twins*, London: Hodder and Stoughton, 1963, p. 47.

4 Gummer, *The Chavasse Twins*, p. 61.

5 Gummer, *The Chavasse Twins*, p. 63.

6 Jonathan Sacks, *Faith in the Future*, London: Darton, Longman & Todd, 1995, pp. 138–9.

7 Mona Siddiqui, *Hospitality and Islam: Welcoming in God's name*, New Haven and London: Yale University Press, 2015, pp. 12–13.

8 Siddiqui, *Hospitality and Islam*, pp. 124–5.

9 Matthew 5.43–44.

10 Jonathan Sacks, *Not in God's Name: Confronting religious violence*, London: Hodder & Stoughton, 2015, p. 263.

Further reading

1 Because some things are evil

For an academic account of most of the arguments in this Little Book of Guidance see my *Moral Passion and Christian Ethics*, Cambridge: Cambridge University Press, 2017. I am most grateful to Professors Robin Lovin, Stephen Clark, David Martin and Christopher Hallpike and to Dr John Court for their critical help with *Moral Passion* and, in addition, to Philip Law of SPCK and Nick Spencer of Theos for their help with this Little Book.

For a Christian philosophical account of objective evil see Gordon Graham, *Evil and Christian Ethics*, Cambridge: Cambridge University Press, 2001.

2 Because if I scratch your back you will scratch mine

For a recent discussion of connections and discontinuities between evolution and Christian ethics see Martin A. Novak and Sarah Coakley (eds), *Evolution, Games and God*, Cambridge and New York: Cambridge University Press, 2013.

For a recent discussion of the Golden Rule see Harry J. Gensler, *Ethics and the Golden Rule*, New York and London: Routledge, 2013.

3 Because it is our duty

For details of Noel Chavasse's life see Selwyn Gummer, *The Chavasse Twins*, London: Hodder and Stoughton, 1963. For Chavasse family letters see <http://www.spc.ox.ac.uk/about/college-history/francis-chavasse-christopher-chavasse-1904-1919> (accessed 12 October 2015).

For a recent Christian philosophical account of moral obligation see C. Stephen Evans, *God and Moral Obligation*, Oxford: Oxford University Press, 2013.

4 Because God is good

For the opening dilemma about God and goodness (Plato's *Euthyphro* dilemma) see C. Stephen Evans again: *God and Moral Obligation*, Oxford: Oxford University Press, 2013.

Jonathan Sacks, *Faith in the Future*, London: Darton, Longman & Todd, 1995, and *Not in God's Name: Confronting religious violence*, London: Hodder & Stoughton, 2015.

Mona Siddiqui, *Hospitality and Islam: Welcoming in God's name*, New Haven and London: Yale University Press, 2015.